5.50

THE
IDEAL HOME
Book of
InteriorS

THE IDEAL HOME

Book of

Interiors

Peter Douglas and Clive Helm

BLANDFORD PRESS

Poole   **Dorset**

First published in the U.K. 1982 by Blandford Press,
Link House, West Street, Poole, Dorset, BH15 1LL

British Library Cataloguing in Publication Data

Douglas, Peter
  The Ideal home book of interiors.
  1. Interior decoration
  I. Title   II. Helm, Clive
  747   NK2110

Distributed in the United States by
Sterling Publishing Co., Inc.,
2 Park Avenue, New York, N.Y. 10016.

ISBN 0 7137 1093 4

Typeset in 12 on 13½pt V.I.P. Times and printed and
bound in Great Britain by Fakenham Press Limited,
Fakenham, Norfolk

Contents

Foreword

During the sixty-year publishing history of *Ideal Home* magazine, there have been many significant changes in the home-ownership market, not least in decorative styles and materials. Nevertheless, the fundamental desire to improve one's own home remains constant.

In reviewing material for this book, produced in collaboration with Blandford Press, Peter Douglas and I have been conscious of the aim to provide not only the 'best of *Ideal Home*' but also to reproduce homes filled with thought-provoking and inspiring decorative ideas for the reader.

Terence Whelan
Editor, IDEAL HOME magazine

Introduction

This book presents a selection of some of the best features on interior design that have appeared in *Ideal Home* magazine in recent months. In order to give an insight into the purpose of this book I feel I should explain here why I have chosen these particular features and put them together in this way.

In selecting the schemes for this compilation I have tried to include a wide range of homes, ranging from small flats to town houses, country cottages to suburban semis, all owned by people of different age groups and with different needs in mind. Each shows what can be done within the constraints of space, location and available cash to create a home to suit a particular lifestyle, catering for individual needs and preferences.

My intention has been to present homes—be they houses, flats, cottages or mansions—in their 'finished' form, showing what can be done rather than the nuts and bolts of how to do it. This book will not tell you how to knock down a wall or build a new kitchen unit but it can show you how various combinations of colour, lighting, textures and space can be used to create an aesthetically pleasing yet functional home.

Having seen what can be done by others, I suggest that readers should have no hesitation in copying these ideas. By this I do not mean slavishly following every colour or nuance shown in a particular scheme or illustration, but picking the best from a number of schemes and adapting them to your own tastes and needs. Feel free to copy other people's ideas and then inject some individual touch of your own.

Although many of the features here reflect contemporary trends, in particular the current preference for 'natural' materials such as wood, brick and tiles, and strong, plain colours such as browns, reds and greens, the schemes are not strictly contemporary in the popular sense. Rather they represent a pleasing blend of styles ancient and modern, showing how old and new can be made to harmonise. This is the true skill of the modern interior designer, the ability to introduce the latest in furniture and décor, blending modern lines and colour with the existing fabric of the house and yet retaining the individual characteristics of an older building.

In all the cases I have selected for this book I have been impressed by the innate sense of style displayed by the owners. They show that instinctive feel for how a particular colour scheme or grouping of furniture may or may not work, without having to follow a strict rule book. There are, of course, certain general guidelines relating to the use of colour, texture and lighting and although these are not always expressly referred to in the text they can be learned by studying the various schemes in this book.

Virtually all these interiors were created by the owners themselves without the use of professional help, although builders and other specialists were used where necessary for some skilled jobs. Many of the couples spent two years or more creating their homes, devoting every moment of their spare time to renovation, decorating and furnishing. House conversion is not something to be entered into lightly and I would advise anyone considering it to make sure that they are fully aware of all the potential problems and the work needed before taking it on. It is a time consuming and often frustrating task, demanding absolute dedication and a great deal of hard work, although, of course, extremely rewarding in the end.

As I have said, these are all homes designed to be lived in by specific individuals or families, catering for individual tastes and lifestyles. However, I hope that every reader will find something to inspire or imitate or adapt to his or her own particular situation.

I would like to thank the people whose homes are featured, for their time and patience in answering my questions and allowing us to visit and photograph their homes, and photographer Clive Helm whose excellent pictures more than make up for the inadequacy of words when displaying the final results of their efforts.

Peter Douglas

A Musician's Family Home

This is a large, converted Victorian family house situated opposite a common in South London. Its owner is a professional musician and composer, so that the house is called upon to fulfil many functions. In addition to providing a family home for the owner, his wife, two lively children and a selection of dogs and cats, the house also incorporates a basement recording studio where the owner does a lot of his work. Nearly all the alterations were carried out by the owners themselves and show what can be done with a lot of determination and a consistent sense of style.

When the owners decided to move from their first, rather cramped home, they had a number of priorities in mind that helped them choose this large house and its location facing an unspoilt park. Among these priorities was a need to provide sufficient room to grow and a place for both the owner and his wife to do much of their work. They also wanted a garden—essential where children are around—and plenty of room for entertaining and for offering overnight accommodation to

Light filters into the wide, welcoming entrance hall through carefully restored stained glass panels. All the woodwork has been stripped of paint and left in its natural state.

guests and friends. They also needed space in which to display a collection of pictures, furniture and Victorian objects gathered together over a number of years.

The end result is a warm, even cluttered environment that perhaps looks its best when half a dozen guests come round for dinner or relaxing drinks around the fireside or in front of the television. The casual visitor would be amazed to find that the household includes two very active children and that the owner's wife, with the aid of an au pair and occasional daily help, manages to keep the house spotless and in perfect order, still finding time for her children, frequent entertaining and her own work as a freelance fashion consultant.

A rambling Victorian pile, the house is built on three floors, with a deceptively narrow exterior. The basement, which consisted of little more than a small cellar when the family moved in, has been extended to provide a working room for the owner and a fully sound-proofed recording studio to help him in his work as a songwriter and record producer.

One of the ways to treat a large living room such as this, which has been converted from two smaller rooms, is to create separate zones for sitting and relaxing, listening to music or watching television. This end of the room at the front of the house provides a conversation area dominated by the impressive black slate fireplace.

The ground floor has been opened up and three distinct areas created—a large living room which extends from the front of the house to the conservatory, a kitchen with a dining area attached, and a conservatory which is the linking element between these two. The conservatory was built by the owner himself with the help of a local builder and created out of an abandoned corner of the garden between the living room and the kitchen. Other structural work included removal of a dividing wall that separated the two halves of the new living room and the erection of a rolled steel joist to replace the dividing wall. Because this was a load bearing wall the supporting columns had to be extended right down into the basement.

A former scullery has been transformed into the kitchen. This is quite small and consists of a clever arrangement of built-in units, which between them contain a hob, an eye-level oven, an automatic dishwasher and plenty of storage space. The central heating boiler was originally sited here but to give more space it was transferred to the basement. Above the four burner hob is a corner canopy, constructed by the owner using rough plaster on a plywood base. This conceals an extractor fan that removes cooking smells and vents them through an outside wall. A hinged flap that comes down across the back door provides further temporary working space. Separating the kitchen area from the dining area is an island unit constructed of red brick and pine in which are found the refrigerator and store cupboards on the kitchen side, and the washing machine and drier on the dining side. All these are concealed behind pine louvred doors.

In the dining area itself, a solid pine table provides the setting for cheerful informal family meals, or, with the lights dimmed and candles lit, the correct ambience for sparkling late night dinners. The quarry tiled floor is burnished to a warm red and, almost hidden in a fireplace, there is a delightful antique tiled stove of the sort seen in French country kitchens, which the owners found by chance in a local antique shop. A pine dresser and elegant wooden dining chairs complete the basic furnishings. Colours are kept simple—white for the walls and ceiling, contrasting with the tiled floor and brick and pinewood fitments, and giving a neutral background for the splashes of colour provided by a number of contemporary prints and paintings.

Leading off from the dining area, the large conservatory has white walls and a quarry tiled floor, teamed with a riot of plants and flowers. In this way it provides a natural extension to the ground floor. Here the children can play, toys being returned dutifully to large wicker baskets before they go to bed.

Opposite top: The kitchen is divided into a cooking area and an informal dining room. From the dining end, the cooking section can be seen beyond the louvred pine doors of the dividing wall which houses the refrigerator and washing machine/dryer. An antique French stove is seen on the left.

Opposite bottom: The compact kitchen work area features a built-in hob and separate eye-level oven. A home-made plywood and plaster hood above the hob helps to confine cooking smells which are extracted through a ventilator in the outside wall.

A separate children's bathroom is essential in a busy household such as this. Here, tiled walls take care of splashes behind the bath and wickerwork is used on the side of the bath and on fitments.

The conservatory can also be used to provide an overflow area for entertaining, or a relaxing setting for afternoon tea or embroidery sessions.

The conservatory leads to the living room, which can best be described as cosy and elegant with a touch of eccentricity. The floors consists of wide, stripped wooden boards, which are covered with off-white sheepskin rugs. The walls have been painted with olive green emulsion, and the ceiling is white. The original scheme called for an olive green ceiling but this was found to be too oppressive in practice. One end of the room forms a cosy sitting area with a large leather upholstered chesterfield and a carved Victorian sofa set at right angles. The occasional tables consist of a happy blend of modern glass and chrome with genuine Victorian originals, and a commanding black slate fireplace is given even greater emphasis by the addition of a huge gilt framed mirror placed above it. Plants and flowers are seen in profusion everywhere.

A chaise-longue provides a separate conversation spot at the other end of the room, which is dominated by one of the

owner's spur-of-the-moment purchases in the uncompromising shape of a church organ. This is still in full working order having been rescued from destruction and shipped by lorry from a country church. Books, records and hi-fi equipment are housed in purpose built shelves. Flanking the door into the conservatory is an elegant glass cabinet displaying an interesting collection of snuff boxes and other objects.

The entrance hall is wide and welcoming, with the warmth of rich wood floors and an elegant Victorian hallstand and glass fronted dresser. The front door is panelled in coloured stained glass. A varied collection of pictures lines the walls and leads up the stairs to the first floor landing.

In such a busy household two bathrooms are essential. This requirement influenced the plans for the master bedroom, which was a major conversion job and involved the transformation of a smaller secondary room into the owner's own private bathroom. This whole area is now decorated with a tasteful green patterned wallpaper which contrasts well with the plain beige carpet. The floor to ceiling cupboards covering two

The main bathroom converted from a room adjoining the master bedroom is decorated with the same green wallpaper as the bedroom. An archway constructed by the owner partially conceals the bath itself.

In the master bedroom a wall of cupboards conceals the disused fireplace and provides plenty of space for clothes. An old pub mirror makes an unusual headboard for the bed and is complemented by antique wall lights.

alcoves and a fireplace are also finished in the same paper. A heavy Victorian mirror provides a dramatic headboard for the bed and antique wall lights complete the nineteenth century atmosphere. A dressing table has been made out of a marble covered washstand, with a small escritoire adjacent in which trinkets and letters can be stored. The bathroom is reached through an arched doorway and the bath itself is partially concealed behind a wooden screen that continues the line of the door opening.

The first floor also contains the children's bedroom which doubles as a workroom. Bunk beds take up little space and there is a wall of cupboards housing books, files and musical instruments, reflecting the owners' varied working interests. A huge Italian designed desk, which is adjustable in height and has a sensible white worktop, can be used as a desk or sewing table, or for the layout of children's toys. Toys are kept in wicker baskets or in a series of multi-drawer plastic cubes.

On this floor there is also a tiny nursery, with pale green walls, beige carpet and cheerful striped blinds. Here a small washbasin has been retained and enclosed in a wooden fitment. A separate bathroom lies at the end of the landing and is decorated in brown and beige, with wicker panels enclosing the bathtub itself. Brown glazed tiles cope with children's splashing.

Further upstairs, the house has two more rooms which are used as guest rooms. One of them can double as an extra small living room, complete with its own television set and foldaway bed. Walls and ceilings are white and the sloping roof is in complete contrast to the high ceilings found elsewhere.

The general pressure on space is illustrated by ingenious use of two landing spaces. On one level there is a deep cupboard for clothes, luggage and odds and ends, and on the higher level the owner has sited a desk and work area, complete with all the necessary equipment: extension telephone, typewriter and hi-fi.

Although the house is somewhat narrow overall, its depth is deceptive and with the addition of the conservatory, best use has been made of the available space. Naturally in fine weather, much of the life of the household spills over into the garden, which contains a paved patio area, a lawn and vegetable and fruit garden hidden behind a wall of shrubs. Overhanging trees provide plenty of shade for lazy meals at weekends and an element of privacy.

This is a house that is called upon to perform many functions, and with innate good taste and some clever furnishing ideas, the owners have succeeded in creating a home that is both elegant and comfortable, where the visitor is always sure of a welcome.

A Small Town House
in a Cathedral City

House renovation is rarely without its problems, but the owners of this house appear to have encountered and overcome more than their fair share of difficulties. The result is an elegant three storey home set in the heart of a Cathedral city in the south of England. The couple moved there when they opened a restaurant in a converted Victorian foundry, after living for five years in a country cottage. The serious renovation work took up almost two years and included the installation of central heating, which the owners tackled themselves, and the complete replacement of the downstairs floor.

In a routine examination of the floorboards, the owners found that the joists underneath were thoroughly rotten. Although a local builder first agreed to do the job of replacement, at the last minute he let them down, so the owners decided to tackle the job themselves.

This was not without its problems. For example, one day a whole lorry load of ready mixed concrete was delivered and the young couple found that they had overestimated their requirements by something like 2 cubic yards (1.5 m³). With nowhere else to put it, the extra material was left in the street until the police asked them to move it before it set hard.

The owner's wife admits that she sets extremely high standards for herself and is known locally as something of a demand-

This small living room, which is entered direct from the street, is dramatically but simply furnished with large, solid pieces. The colourful, well padded sofa is set off perfectly against the strong plain colours of the walls and curtains.

The deceptively plain exterior of this terraced town house gives few clues to the delights within. Good use of external colour and attention to window detail make this small house stand out from its neighbours.

ing shopper. Accordingly her choice of furnishings includes kitchen units which were delivered all the way from Germany and much of the furniture, including a brass bed, from various shops in London. This bed in particular caused a number of problems. When they found that it would not go in through the window, the owners decided that the only way to get it to the bedroom was to cut away the banisters and carry it up the stairs. Only when this had been done was it discovered that the bed itself could be taken to pieces!

Another colourful incident involved the delivery at the same time of no fewer than three separate suites, as the couple were unable to decide which one they wished to purchase. With the aid of a helpful driver each one was lifted out of the delivery van and installed in the living room temporarily, before they could make up their minds which one to buy. Surprisingly, local shops are now becoming used to their unusual requests.

In spite of the many frustrations connected with the conversion and decoration of this property, the result is a cosy and

One of the many carefully planned purchases was this huge brass bedstead which dominates the main bedroom. The use of a large mirror gives an illusion of space in what is a relatively small room and the colourful patchwork quilt contrasts with the plain walls and carpet.

elegant town house. A number of inside walls have been removed, opening up the entire ground floor so that the front door opens direct from the street into the main living room with a dining area and kitchen beyond.

The furniture that was eventually chosen consists of extremely comfortable armchairs which originally came from America and a large matching sofa. There is little other furniture in this room, and the owners have resisted the temptation to fill the small space with a number of unnecessary items. Objects such as the television set are simply placed on the floor. A coffee coloured carpet has been used throughout the ground floor and helps to unify the different areas.

The kitchen is rather long and narrow and has been brightened considerably with the use of blue, mauve and pink Italian ceramic floor tiles. The kitchen units are brown laminated and reach right up to the ceiling. This part of the house has been

Tiled throughout in Italian ceramics, this bathroom provides a good example of a well thought out colour scheme with careful attention to detail. This is enhanced by clever use of natural and artificial lighting.

23

The guest room need not become a repository for unwanted furniture: this simply furnished bedroom is immediately welcoming and put together with the comfort of visitors in mind.

extended to provide a small outdoor patio and a separate laundry room which is reached from outside.

The first floor consists of the main bedroom and bathroom. The bathroom has again been tiled in Italian ceramic, and this contrasts with the gold plated fittings and simple pine cupboards. The main bedroom is dominated by the comfortable brass bed and is given an illusion of space by the addition of a huge mirror to one of the walls. The walls have deliberately been left plain.

Similar treatment has been applied to two smaller bedrooms on the floor above, one of which is used by the owner's daughter and the other left spare for guests. Again the walls are plain, as is the carpet, and the only splashes of colour are provided by the bedspreads, flowers and plants, and the occasional picture or ornament.

One interesting feature of the house is the absence of ceiling lights. This was a deliberate policy of the owners who prefer to use table lamps to cast an interesting variety of shapes and shadows. In the kitchen the temptation to install strip lighting was resisted, and instead a number of directional spot-lamps have been used to good effect.

This house has been designed and furnished to suit the lifestyle of its owners. With little time to spend on cleaning or even relaxing, the house has been deliberately designed to be easy to maintain and to provide a relaxing haven after a busy day. The owners, however, describe themselves as inveterate house converters and would be quite willing to sell up, move on and repeat the process all over again.

Careful Conversion of a Listed Building

Moving from a small modern house to one that was built 150 years ago is not without its problems, but this is just what one young London couple did when they decided to move into their new home some four years ago. The move was prompted by the need for more space for living and working (one of the owners is a freelance writer) and the need for a garden and room in which to bring up a young family. The result was a large rambling house in the Blackheath area of South London, reputedly one of several built for Nelson's admirals.

Because the house is a grade 2 listed building, major alterations to the exterior are not permitted. However, considerable improvement has been carried out inside, which consists of a basement and three floors.

The owners decided that the basement area, which was originally little more than a cellar with small windows looking out to the front and back, would be just right for a large kitchen and dining room. The rest of the house had been divided into two separate flats, an arrangement which proved quite useful

A sunken patio, leading off the basement kitchen/diner, was constructed by removing vast amounts of soil; a task which the owners undertook themselves. This not only provides a delightful brick and paved area for sunny morning breakfasts but also reduces the problems of damp at the back of the house.

during the period of the alterations as the couple were able to live in one of the former flats while working on another section of the house. Some money for improvements was available from the local authority and the period of conversion was spread over two years. The owners did all the work themselves with a little help from friends, although a local builder was called in to do the more skilled work such as repointing the brickwork.

One of the first major tasks concerned the basement, where a dividing wall had to be demolished and the garden end excavated to form a sunken patio area, with access from the kitchen by way of glass sliding doors. The area that had to be dug out measured some 12 × 8 ft (4 × 2.5 m) and was mostly 7 ft (2 m) deep of solid earth. Every weekend for a period of four months the couple dug out this area by hand, filling a number of skips in the process. Unfortunately access to the garden was too narrow to allow the use of a wheelbarrow so the whole back-

The kitchen, converted from a dark basement room, looks out onto the patio. Plenty of daylight and a feeling of space has been achieved as the room virtually extends into the garden. Nearly all the cupboards and appliances are built in, thus removing clutter.

Above: The dining end of the former basement can be cleared by taking apart the modern compressed board table. The cork floor and pine cladding lend warmth, offset by plain white paintwork.

Opposite: A warm welcome from the owners' young daughter at the front door. Good use of plain colours on the walls and floor accentuate the grand proportions of the doorway and stairs.

breaking operation was carried out using buckets.

Other problems encountered included a flood that inundated the basement and a near disastrous fire when the adhesive used for laying the cork tiles caught alight, sparked off by the pilot light on the newly installed gas boiler. Despite these setbacks, the final result is a pleasant airy and spacious home with plenty of windows, white walls and wood or cork throughout.

Throughout the house there is a marked absence of clutter, and most rooms are very sparsely furnished. This is the owners' personal choice as they do not feel a need to fill up every available space with pieces of furniture. The layout of the house has also proved to be very practical: the couple like to entertain and sometimes the basement area has been turned into a disco for fifty or more while the less energetic retire to the huge ground floor living area. By locating his study in the former second floor attic, the writing half of this partnership finds that he can cut himself off to work when he has a need for peace and quiet. Books, telephone and typewriter are all close to hand while a telephone intercom keeps him in touch with each floor of the house.

The major conversion work took about two years to complete and the couple have spent a further two years decorating

Left: Moving the kitchen/diner to the basement meant that virtually the whole of the ground floor could be opened up into this large living area. The owners have retained the feeling of space by furnishing with a few, well chosen, low-level pieces.

Below: A simple pine cupboard has been transformed by the use of patterned wall-coverings which can be changed when they lose their freshness.

and doing the remaining jobs. These consist of things like fixing tiles and installing lighting track; the sort of thing that you do not do immediately but which has to be done in order to bring the house to its completed state.

Starting from the bottom, the house consists of the basement area converted from old cellars into a pleasant kitchen, dining and family room, which leads out to the sunken patio and garden. On the ground floor are the entrance hall, a small cloakroom and a large living room which has been converted from two smaller rooms. The main bedroom and children's bedroom and bathroom are situated on the first floor, while the second floor has an attic, used for storage, and the owner's study and workroom.

The patio, which was dug out of bare earth, is now a delightful brick and paved area, with steps containing plants, flowers and plenty of greenery. Removing the earth from the side of the house has also had the effect of reducing problems of dampness in what was formerly a basement.

A good view of the patio is seen from the kitchen through the two glass sliding doors. Here cork tiles have been laid on the floor and the ceiling clad with pine planks. Nearly all the furniture is built-in with the exception of a working kitchen table—also used for informal meals—and a petal-shaped dining table at the other end of the room, which when not in use can be folded flat and hung against a wall to look like a contemporary sculpture. The dining chairs are, in fact, made of compressed cardboard. This part of the basement also features built-in units, and leading off from it are further storage rooms and the laundry area.

Nearly the whole of the ground floor is taken up with the huge living room, which is furnished with stunning simplicity. Walls and ceiling are severely plain, as is the close fitted carpet, and beyond a number of comfortable low chairs and occasional tables the room has very little furniture. It is the ideal place in which to relax and entertain friends. The somewhat severe approach adopted by the owners is partially relieved by the use of plants and flowers almost everywhere.

The main bedroom is again another model of simplicity, with its stripped pine floors and general absence of clutter. Here furnishings consist only of the bed itself and a pine chest of drawers. White blinds are used at the windows and the walls and ceiling are also white.

Pine cladding is also used in the bathroom, contrasted with a white wall and tiled surfaces on the floor and bath surround. The children's bedroom is made colourful with the use of bright primary colours on the double bunk bed and other furniture

Opposite top: Bunk beds in cheerful primary colours add excitement for the children and save space in their bedroom which can be used for playing and hobbies.

Opposite bottom: Once again furniture is kept to a minimum in the master bedroom. The wide pine planks of the floor were considered too good to cover and there is plenty of warmth and colour here in spite of plain walls and window blinds.

Above: Pine cladding is used to good effect in the bathroom, contrasting well with white enamelware and blind. Note the continuation of the floor tiles part way up the bath.

Above right: The owner's study retreat at the top of the house is a well organised work area with telephone intercom to other floors, and ensures privacy when required.

used for toy storage.

At the top of the house, the study is decorated in shades of brown and white and features a home-made desk and shelving units designed for quiet and efficient work.

This treatment amply illustrates the fact that it is not necessary to fill up a house with objects and that it is possible to let the lightness and space of a delightful old building work well on their own. This sort of approach can be adopted by young couples possibly furnishing their home for the first time, although in this case it is part of the owners' deliberate policy.

A
Cornish
Farmhouse

Above: An arched doorway and window give a slightly church-like appearance to this lovingly restored Cornish farmhouse.

Below: In the main living room the stone of the chimney breast has been exposed and left natural around the open fireplace, and the traditional flagstones, taken up in order to put in a damp proof membrane, have been relaid.

Taking the decision to leave a comfortable London home and an established business connection is one that the owner of this house does not regret. A creative consultant by profession, he is now firmly established in a renovated farmhouse on the edge of a moor, and finds it difficult to recall the days when the countryside was little more than the view across Clapham Common.

He found the house almost by accident, while staying with friends in a nearby village. It is one of several built about the middle of the last century by a well known local landowner, whose insignia still adorns a stained glass window illuminating the unusual curved wooden staircase. Looking through old records, the present owner discovered that a house had stood on this site for more than 600 years and that its name, 'Lanxon', in the Cornish language means either a monastery or a farm enclosure. This possibly gives some clue to the house's slightly church-like exterior, with its stained glass and stark carved stone cross.

Inside, the owner has created a comfortable home and workplace for himself and two amiable cats. Not unexpectedly, he found that the building did not have a damp course, but he overcame this problem by raising the flagstones and laying

concrete and a damp proof membrane beneath. A dividing wall has also been removed to open up two ground floor rooms and the loft was insulated.

The rest of the work consisted largely of decorating and stripping the woodwork, all of which had been painted with several layers of dark brown. The walls had been limewashed occasionally, but little real work had been done on the house for several decades, and it showed.

Throughout, the owner has been at pains to preserve the best of the original fabrics, so that the downstairs slate slab flooring is only covered with occasional rugs and some of the walls have been left natural and exposed. One of the fireplaces had been filled in, but persistent digging was rewarded by an impressive arched hearth which now houses a wood burning stove.

The main ground floor room divides itself naturally into a dining and living area. The dining end is furnished with a

Above left: The original builder of this house has left his trademark in the delightful stained glass window which illuminates the stairs.

Above right: An efficient woodburning stove has been installed in the fireplace of a small ground floor room.

traditional solid pine table, bentwood chairs and a tall pine dresser housing an impressive display of china. The living end of the room features a selection of comfortable sofas and easy chairs, grouped around a large open fireplace.

Plants are used in abundance to soften the harsh lines of the stonework and exposed wooden beams. Shaded tablelamps are usually used to provide lighting but a centre light, with a Chinese paper shade, can be used for more general illumination. For a change of scene, or if he does not wish to warm up the main living room, the owner has the choice of a second, smaller room at the rear of the house. Here white painted walls and a ceiling of white painted boards and exposed beams are in contrast to the larger living room. Furniture consists of a few solid pieces and a delightful pine window seat. Heating here is also by a wood burning stove.

A slate floor and quarry tiled work surface are the main features of the kitchen, while pine shelves expose an array of kitchenware. The refrigerator, freezer and electric cooker are virtually the only modern touches.

In the main bedroom, a pine floor and pine framed mirror contrast well with the colourful hand knitted patchwork cover. The views over the surrounding countryside are impressive. In a guest room the owner has constructed an ingenious wardrobe consisting of a light wood frame and panels cut out from slatted

Opposite top left: A delightful pine framed window in the smaller living room provides a seat for a view over the moors from the back of the house.

Opposite top right: The dining area at one end of the main living room features a beautiful solid pine table matching the wooden shutters of the window.

Opposite bottom left: In the main bedroom home-made cupboards consist of slatted bamboo blinds attached to a light wooden frame.

Opposite bottom right: Here in the bathroom the owner's artistic urges got the better of him.

39

bamboo blinds. A result is an unobtrusive but very practical structure.

The large bathroom has been given a touch of the exotic, with an impressive mural featuring all kinds of marine life which runs across two whole walls. Cork tiles have been used extensively to provide warmth, with stencilled petal designs giving a touch of originality. A large airing cupboard hides plumbing and tank and the use of natural materials generally has not detracted from the house's period style.

The owner works in a studio on the first floor, overlooking fields, woods and the moor beyond. Although the pace of life is less hectic than when he was established in London, he has gained a useful reputation locally as a commercial designer and can happily combine his professional life with the enjoyment of country pursuits such as riding and walking.

Here he says that he can enjoy more space and peace than was possible in London. So much so that visits to London are a real nightmare now.

Small Scale Comfort

Above: A beautiful front door, carefully restored and waxed, gives a clue to the attention to detail applied by the owners to the rest of the house.

Right: A solid suburban terrace house, typical of many in the area, and increasingly sought by enterprising young couples like the owners.

Buying one's first home is an important decision, but one young couple, he American and she Swedish, set about finding their home with typical transatlantic efficiency, taking just one week to find exactly what they wanted.

Tired of house-hunting part-time, they set themselves one week in which to find the house of their dreams and in this time looked at some sixty properties. Unfortunately, their first choice was snapped up by some other eager young couple, but instead of despairing at this they followed the golden rule of all home buyers: they persevered in the unshaken belief that the house they really wanted was just around the corner. Sure enough it was, and they do not regret having lost the race for the first property.

The state of the building was what they euphemistically described as 'raw'. The property had not been lived in for some time and had been basically renovated before being put on the market. It was painted throughout in one colour, and most of the walls were covered in a rough textured wallpaper which the couple spent many agonising hours removing. Although the building had been replumbed and rewired, there was no kitchen, heating or carpets. Totally inexperienced in these matters, the couple moved from a rented flat in a fashionable quarter of central London to this, their first real home in the suburbs. However, they were motivated by a desire for more space and the feeling of independence that a rented flat simply

Above left: An example of solid comfort in the living room, with a cheerful log fire set in an impressive modern brass surround.

Above right: Neutral shades of beige and buttermilk used throughout the hall, stairs and landing form a linking element between the floors.

A white painted ceiling and tall, pleated curtains help add height to this comparatively small living room. Particular attention has been given to lighting with ceiling downlights supplemented by elegant free-standing reading lamps.

could not bring. The formalities of transferring property took an amazingly brief five weeks, after which builders took over for two months, followed by a further two months in the hands of the decorators. This time scale must be something of a record for property conversion.

Like many similar properties in the area, mainly Victorian or early 1920s housing, the building consisted of a large number of small rooms which the couple proceeded to open up. The house has three floors and a basement. On the ground floor is a large living area and kitchen, the living room being converted from two smaller rooms. On the first floor are the principal bedroom, an American style den for watching television, a bathroom, separate w.c. and a laundry room, which they plan eventually to turn into a photographic darkroom. On the top floor the couple have created a guest room which has its own bathroom, and there is also an attic at present reached through

the bathroom but which presents exciting possibilities for the future.

The couple have chosen a distinctive modern style of décor, with a pleasant mixture of greens, beige, white and buttermilk as linking elements throughout the house. The ground floor living room has dark green walls, a white painted ceiling and beige carpeting and curtains. Built-in fitted shelves and cupboards are also painted dark green and highlighted against this background is a striking brass fireplace slightly raised off the ground. Furnishings are deliberately simple and solid, consisting of a maroon upholstered sofa and a chair with an interesting checkered cover. There are plenty of plants, brass lamps and a well-proportioned glass topped coffee table, and prints and other objects are highlighted by ceiling spotlights. The use of floor-to-ceiling curtains at the windows accentuates the height of this room.

A quiet corner for work or study, overlooking the rear garden, is decorated with a clever contrast of dark brown walls and white paintwork.

Above: The efficient and well appointed kitchen is divided into a cooking area and dining section by a low island unit. Again clever use of lighting illuminates work surfaces and sink

Opposite: The shower room features a specially raised wash basin to accommodate the tall owner and a smoked glass shower cabinet edged with chrome. The walls are covered with unusual brown and cream tiles.

The kitchen has been divided into two sections, for eating and preparation, with a low level unit that extends partway across this long, fairly narrow room. The natural materials such as cork and quarry tiles that have been chosen contrast well with the dark red walls and are relieved by the white ceiling. The round dining table is oak and teams well with the dark upholstered chairs. Cabinets and shelves have been stained to blend in. Modern appliances consisting of a large fridge-freezer, dishwasher and oven, do not obtrude, the fridge-freezer being a pleasant brown shade.

A considerable amount of work space has been allowed in the kitchen, with a double stainless steel sink and drainer. An extractor hood over the hob and oven efficiently removes cooking odours whilst spotlights are used effectively to illuminate the work surfaces. The kitchen leads out to the garden, a concession to their lifestyles which leave little time for housework.

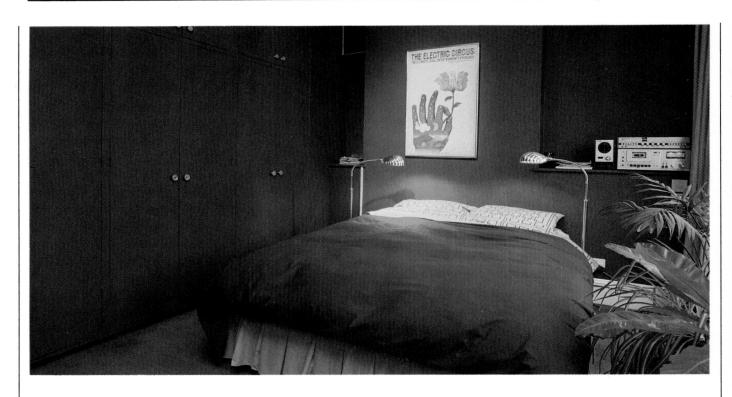

Simplicity is the keynote of the bedroom, with built-in cupboards to conceal clothes, reaching from floor to ceiling. Dark, restful colours are used.

The principal bedroom echoes many of the features of the living room, the same dark green has been used on the walls, and built-in cupboards, with white used on the ceiling. The carpeting is also green. These colours are reflected again in the brown duvet, beige bedlinen and the patterned Laura Ashley curtains. Apart from the bed and a simple pine chest, a wall of cupboards is the main feature of this room. Inside they are a model of orderliness with wire baskets fitted as pull out drawers.

The shower room is a predominantly masculine domain. Here we find brown and cream wall tiles, mahogany woodwork and dark brown cork tiled floor. Even the height of the washbasin has been raised to accommodate the owner's 6 ft (183 cm) frame. The shower cabinet is a streamlined affair of chrome and smoked glass.

The second floor guest room and bathroom are rather more pretty in contrast to much of the simpler décor in other parts of the house.

Throughout this small and compact house the varying elements are brought together with the use of buttermilk walls and ceilings and beige carpeting, used principally in the hall, landings and stairs. This approach helps to coordinate the contrasting styles found at the different levels of the building. The result is a satisfying blend of American flair, Swedish efficiency and old English charm.

A Country Cottage in Town

When a husband refuses to live more than ten minutes from his city office and his wife yearns for a country cottage, it might seem like a problem with no solution. However, a pair of London designers achieved a glorious compromise in the purchase of a 120-year-old, two storey cottage standing in an acre of garden in a busy suburb only five minutes from the office where they both work.

The couple found the property entirely by accident, while driving down a little-known street, and as soon as they saw it they realised it was just what they wanted: a town house in a country setting, or a country home right in the heart of town. Either way it could not have been a better choice.

With a small, flower filled front garden and large sloping lawns to the rear, the solid, brick built house enjoys almost complete seclusion. A modern block of flats behind is partially screened by a wall of trees and a small river runs alongside the edge of the garden.

The house itself consists of a cellar, ground and first floors.

More in the style of a country cottage than a town house, this delightful sitting room is actually in the heart of a London home. French doors lead to a garden, around which flows a stream.

Although the cellar is too low to be used for anything except storage, the central heating boiler has been conveniently located there, and the couple have also taken advantage of this space by sinking hi-fi speakers into the floor of the living room above.

The living room is a working example of how old and modern furniture can blend happily in the right setting. The reason for this choice of furniture was partly accidental, as the couple came from a modern house and simply could not afford to throw everything away. The contrasting styles blend well with each other and the room, with its ample fireplace and full length French doors leading to the garden, offers a warm and welcoming atmosphere for occupants and guests alike. Light carpeting and a delicately patterned wallpaper, used throughout the house, successfully counterbalance the heavyweight but restful sofa and armchairs. Nearby are neat storage racks for

This quite large kitchen features an island hob unit with specially raised sides to prevent accidents or spills. The cupboards and work surfaces are solid, natural wood.

The dining room also overlooks the garden and can accommodate eight or more guests for dinner in an informal atmosphere enhanced by the bright tablecloth and collection of unusual signs on the walls.

cassettes and headphones, as well as an ultramodern sculptured lamp, reflecting the couple's interest in distinctively modern design.

Leading off the living room is a completely country style dining room. Here are pine floors and a pine dresser, bentwood chairs and a bright tablecloth that dispel any feelings of formality. Another whimsical touch is the collection of pub signs and posters scattered across several walls. These contrast with an elegant Chinese painting which dominates the remaining wall and faces the window overlooking the garden.

The kitchen is also in traditional farmhouse style with a central unit forming the focal point. This specially designed fitment is made of solid pine with a brass work surface and recessed gas hob. Raised edges on three sides make for safety and a neat appearance. Other units were bought ready made. The floor tiles are vinyl, further evidence of the owners' faith in modern materials. The kitchen has been designed so that two people can work in it at once and the room can also cope with large family meals and entertaining.

A small study, furnished with bookshelves and a round library table, completes the ground floor accommodation.

Below and opposite: Old and new live happily side by side in this house, reflecting the owners'—who are designers—bold approach to furnishing. In the living room (**below**) hi-fi speakers are concealed beneath the floor, while upstairs corridors (**opposite top**) have all the charm of an old fashioned country hotel. The use of the same patterned wallpaper virtually throughout this large house gives a sense of continuity.

Opposite: All the bedrooms are simply but comfortably furnished with luxurious shag pile carpeting and colourful bedspreads. In the master bedroom (**top**) an ornate carved screen from a church serves as a headboard.

Below: In this small bathroom a sense of elegant luxury is achieved through the partially sunk bath and concealed lighting. The room is made to look larger by the use of mirrors.

The first floor consists of a master bedroom, bathroom and two bedrooms for family and guests. An ornately carved screen, rescued from a church that was about to be demolished, has taken on a new lease of life as a headboard. The owners' bedroom is deliberately kept free of clutter, with clothes stored in fitted cupboards in an adjoining separate dressing room.

A small but comfortable bathroom makes best use of available space by means of a raised platform extending across one wall, into which a traditional deep bath has been sunk. This whole area is close carpeted. A cheerful seaside print lends an outdoor atmosphere and a full length mirror placed sideways above the bath adds further to the feeling of spaciousness. An extractor fan in the sloping ceiling deals effectively with steam, and lighting is concealed behind a horizontal panel.

Throughout the house the couple have deliberately tried to maintain an early nineteenth century atmosphere in their choice of wallpaper and off-white paintwork. Very little structural work has been undertaken, which is not surprising when you learn that the house was converted by a builder for his own residence. The couple find that they appreciate the restful atmosphere after returning from a busy day at the office. There,

The Oriental influence displayed in this spare bedroom fits in with the delicate wallpaper.

because they work with modern designs and materials, everything is up to the minute in appearance. Coming home to a 120-year-old cottage is very relaxing. They say that their present home reflects their more mature taste, in contrast to their former home which was an architect designed wooden house, considered so far ahead of its time that it was featured in a number of magazines. Now that they are older, they confess, they feel they can afford to be a little less dramatic in their approach to living.

A Town House
in the Country

Opposite: The kitchen and informal dining room are designed very much with children in mind. The dining table can be used for homework or games while the owner supervises. Work surfaces are planned for large scale meal preparation in this lively household and plenty of storage space has been provided.

Below: The comfortable living room overlooks the garden and has the air of a town house rather than a spacious country home. Good strong colours are used on the walls and ceiling, relieved by the delicacy of the white drapes.

This house is one of contradictions. Its rural location close to Dartmoor would suggest the ideal country house, and yet its position in a busy village street and its elegant interior furnishings clearly stamp it as a town house. Built on three floors, with two separate staircases, and rooms that range from cosy attic to well proportioned living rooms, the house has been decorated throughout in an exciting and imaginative manner.

Because of the presence of a large garden and the fact that the household includes three active children and a dog, the kitchen/diner and the adjoining conservatory are important elements in the family's daily life and have therefore been designed for informal meals, hobbies, homework and watching television. This whole area is linked with one of the three main entrances and is used for most of the family's comings and goings.

Sensibly, the owners opted for a practical kitchen/dining area, large enough to cater for guests and family meals. The theme here is basically pine units covered in dull red laminate worktops that can be cleaned with a wipe. Counter level units divide the room into its cooking and eating areas, and on the kitchen side, which is placed so that the owner can keep a

watchful eye on the activities of the two youngest children, there is a refrigerator, dishwasher, ample cupboards and sink.

The kitchen/dining area, as well as the more formal dining room next door, has a vivid black and white tiled floor and white walls, while as a contrast, the same dull red as the working surfaces has been used on the ceilings and one wall. A television stands on a long white painted bench which can also be used for seating and storage, while the rest of the furniture is in pine.

The remainder of the ground floor consists of an elegant entrance hall, a large living room overlooking the garden, and the formal dining room. A washing and drying room and a small study, just off the hall, are close to the stairs leading to yet another entrance.

While entertaining, the owners make use of their impressive dining room, with its dark oak table, chairs and dresser. Mirrors are used effectively along one wall to accentuate the room's size, and to reflect the trailing plants growing in the entrance porch seen through a window opposite.

A cheerful open fire is the focal point of the living room, with added warmth provided by the brown painted walls and ceiling and brown carpet. The fireplace wall is in cream rough cast plaster. On one side of the fireplace the alcove has been

A bathroom has been carved out of the main bedroom and is partially concealed by saloon-style doors.

One of several staircases, this one rises majestically from the main entrance hall and the owners have done justice to its proportions with the addition of an elegant chandelier-style light. Again, strong colours on the walls and ceiling contrast with the flimsy white curtains.

The main bedroom, combining cool greens and the warmth of pine woodwork, has an en suite bathroom.

filled with bookshelves, whilst on the other side is a door leading to the conservatory, whose creeping vines can be glimpsed through the door's curtained window. A large sofa and chairs, covered in a patterned fabric and piled with cushions, simply invite relaxation. The presence of a piano, a collection of stuffed birds and—in an adjacent porch leading to the garden—an old church organ, all testify to the owners' varied interests and indicate once more that this is a busy family house.

Flimsy white drapes were chosen for the curtains in the living room, as well as for the landing of the main entrance hall. Here the theme of white wood and brown walls has been repeated and an impressive stairway leads upwards from the original tiled floor, where a charming chaise-longue covered in midnight blue velvet is situated.

The master bedroom is a mixture of cool greens and rich pine woodwork. Apple green walls contrast well with the darker shade of the carpet, while crisp white curtains and bedspread add a summery touch even on the dullest of days. An antique pine desk serves as a dressing table and the clutter of clothes and other possessions is concealed behind louvred pine cupboards, reaching up to the ceiling.

The owners have wisely added a private bathroom en suite, far removed from the clamour of the rest of the household. Here the white bath and basin contrast with a pale orange and mauve wallpaper and a vivid orange shag pile rug. Louvred bar saloon doors separate this from the bedroom.

Although large by most standards, the house is nonetheless designed for efficient running.

Masculine Flair
in Suburbia

Buttermilk emulsion in the entrance hall and on the stairs, and a beige stair carpet extending on to the landing form a link between the varying styles used in this house.

Both as a home and as a workplace, this elegant house fulfils its two purposes with a superb blend of practicality and panache, which do credit to its owner, an American businessman based in London, but working internationally.

The house is a smart, two storey suburban terraced building which, from the outside, looks very much like all the other houses in the street, with its deep red brick and startling white painted eaves and window surrounds. However, once you step inside, you witness a clever and unusual transformation.

Now settled in England, the owner tackled the move from a rambling mansion flat in central London with traditional American efficiency. He first viewed the house in April, was finally installed by October and the only question he asks himself is why it all took so long. Readers familiar with the problems associated with 'having the builders in' will doubtless marvel at the speed with which this house underwent a veritable transformation. The owner describes the state it was in as derelict, with rising damp some 4 ft ($1\frac{1}{2}$ m) up the walls, which all had to be treated and replastered. In addition, some of the outside walls had to be repointed and a lot of hardboard was removed that had been used to cover doors and a part of the stairs. Additional problems were rewiring, plumbing and decorating.

Contracts for the sale were exchanged in September and the owner set a date for moving in. After this had been postponed twice, he finally announced that as owner of a new home, he was fed up with paying rent on a flat as well and he intended to move in. The builders were still working and he and his family in fact lived with them for another four weeks. Most of his belongings were scattered among forty tea chests and for six weeks the owner and his family virtually camped out inside their new house. The day they arrived all the window panes in the sitting room had been removed to make way for new patio doors and the first night was spent with a gaping hole covered only with blankets. At the time London was suffering from frequent power cuts which all added to the difficulties.

Meanwhile, the owner had to continue his work as a graphic designer and one of his biggest disappointments, he recalls, was returning from overseas business trips expecting to find work completed, only to discover that further delays and difficulties had presented themselves. However, by Christmas they were more or less clear of the builders and he was so exhausted by it all that he was forced to take several weeks off work.

Was it all worth it? The answer must be an emphatic yes. The house is two storeys high with the ground floor consisting of a sitting room, dining room with connecting kitchen and utility

room and, at the front of the house, the owner's study. Upstairs are the owner's own bedroom and bedrooms for two of his four children, the others having grown up and left home.

By using buttermilk emulsion paint on the walls and beige carpeting in the hall and upstairs landing, a visual link is at once provided between the different areas of the house, which individually present some quite startling contrasts. However, they manage to work because the job of coordinating the different areas has been done well.

Buttermilk emulsion has been used on the walls and ceiling of the pleasant lounge. French doors occupy almost the whole of one wall, overlooking a red brick patio and gardens beyond. Beige carpeting has been used, with the addition of a bright rug, and main furnishings consist of a huge sofa covered in deep brown cord and a comfortable old wing chair. There are also masses of plants, an old pub table that serves as a desk, and plenty of carefully positioned, colourful pictures on the walls.

The dining room and adjoining kitchen present a complete contrast. Here the walls are painted in a coppery red colour and the ceilings are white. Cork tiles are laid on the floors. The dining table is made of solid pine and a glass fronted pine chest holds plates and glasses.

The kitchen is reached down a couple of steps and is compact and well planned. It was decided not to screen off this area from the dining room and this has resulted in a sense of

Above left: The comfortable living room overlooks the patio and garden. The air of solid, masculine taste conferred by the dark brown cord covered sofa and armchair is lightened by the splashes of bright colour in the prints and cushions.

Above right: A kitchen designed for workmanlike efficiency with plenty of cupboard space. The colour scheme matches that of the adjacent dining room.

space achieved by leaving the two areas open. Units, which reach almost to ceiling height, are finished in warm wood veneers, highlighted by ceiling spotlights.

A former lean-to bathroom has been gutted to make a utility room, complete with washer, dryer and additional large sink, and an extra downstairs w.c.

The owner has created several work areas inside his new home and when he is not writing at a small desk in his bedroom, he makes use of a study situated at the front of the house on the ground floor. Here a rust coloured carpet contrasts with deep brown walls and a white ceiling. Another wall is covered with photographs, prints and other family mementos, recalling the owners' many talents—including photography and play-writing.

The large desk, in ash, is clear of clutter and papers, and files are carefully stored in a row of gleaming cabinets beneath the bay window. A pigeon-hole unit above the desk came from the kitchen of the owner's former flat, as he thought it was too useful to throw away. A piano, television and comfortable cord

The dining room works equally well for informal meals or for entertaining.

covered sofa complete the furnishings of this well planned retreat.

Upstairs are bedrooms for the children and the master bedroom, a large room with another area set aside for quiet creative work. Here again the décor represents a complete change of theme, the dominant colour being a rich blue used on the ceiling and paintwork, while the walls are finished in buttermilk. Greens and blues feature in the tartan fitted carpet, and prints and playbills add still more colour to the walls. The furniture is again of solid pine and well stocked bookshelves are found at each side of the bed.

The bathroom was converted from two smaller rooms and, interestingly, now exists on two levels. Brown tweed carpet is used on the floor, bright green paint on the walls and pale green and cream ceramic tiles surround the bath and shower. The bath and basin are plain white and a rich pine dresser is used to store bathroom paraphernalia.

Although according to its owner the house was not deliber-

In the main bedroom, which includes another work area and plenty of bedtime reading matter, the blue of the tartan carpet is used on the woodwork and ceiling.

Above left: The owner's study, used for writing and listening to music.

Above right: The bathroom is in fact on two levels and was converted from two rooms.

ately planned, it at once presents a warm and welcoming interior that suits his busy international lifestyle. Clearly defined areas for work and relaxation, for eating and preparing meals, greatly contribute to the efficient and smooth running of the household. Altogether it is a good place to come home to.

Young Designers
at Home

Above and opposite top: Two views of the living room of this very individual designers' house. Bold colours and a pleasant mixture of styles work well here, on a budget that was limited. The natural wood floors enhance the sense of light and space.

Opposite below: This detail of the living room shows a display of books and collected toys which add a colourful note.

This house belongs to a young London couple both of whom are involved in the fashion business—one as a designer, the second in promoting the industry. A high degree of comfort and an imaginative flair are the two ingredients which the couple have sought to combine when designing their new home.

As both of them work a full and busy day, they did not have a lot of time for renovation and decorating. The main work took them a period of three years, after which they feel they can relax and enjoy the results of their efforts in a house which offers sufficient space for themselves, two children, a nanny and a dog, who all live together without getting in each other's way.

House-hunting took about eight months, and the couple suffered from the usual problems with builders. Jobs were started and not completed and they ended up doing much of the work themselves. They had a lot of help from their friends, and the major works are now finished, although there are still a couple of rooms which require improvement. The house is built in solid red brick with large sash windows providing plenty of light and an excellent view. The owners are collectors of unusual objects and each room has been given an individual, even exotic touch. However, they have resisted any attempt to provide a particular look or atmosphere and the result is very much a blend of their own individual tastes and style.

The ground floor living room provided plenty of scope for their decorating ideas. It is large and square with a natural wood floor which enhances the sense of light and space. The delicate wallpaper, green and pink stripes against a white background, was first chosen and furnishings kept to a minimum. These consist of large sofas set at right angles and a plate glass and cane coffee table in the centre of the room.

The two sofas, one covered in grey tweed fabric, the other in mustard and brown moquette, dominate the room, but the original fireplace with white wood surround and striking red tiles, provides a splendid focal point. Shelves are used to store a toy collection and the stereo system and books find an orderly home in fitments built in at either side of the fireplace. Dotted around the room are pieces from their toy collection, and in one corner a very convincing pelican perches against a potted plant. Art Deco ornaments and prints add a thirties touch to this room.

The dining room presents a complete contrast. Here the theme is a cool green, from the carpet which was specially dyed, to the delicately patterned wallpaper. Along one wall runs a mirror decorated with jungle scenes and, fitting in with the mood of the room, the French windows at one end lead out into the conservatory and garden beyond.

The contrasting colour scheme in the dining room was chosen to enhance the beauty of this original tiled fireplace.

Furniture again is kept to a minimum, including a round plate glass and chrome dining table with chairs in black and cane. Overhead a round neon light adds a futuristic touch.

This room also boasts a lovely original and unspoilt fireplace decorated with pink and beige tiles, on which sits a cheerful garden gnome.

The entrance hall presents a warm and welcoming appearance, with its natural wooden floorboards and checkered wallpaper as background to a cane occasional table and a giant plant.

The kitchen is rather workman-like, consisting of black floor tiles and black wooden units bought from a showroom display. In vivid contrast, the walls and ceiling have been painted bright yellow and one wall has been cleverly covered in patterned paper showing fruit and vegetables. In keeping with the overall colour scheme, the dining table at one end of the room is in chrome and black, flanked by yellow painted wooden folding chairs, used to save space. A well used pinball machine is much appreciated by the younger members of the family.

The main bedroom is kept deliberately free of clutter and clothes are stored in a separate room using showroom type rail fittings. The only furniture is a double bed, a small chest of drawers and bedside table. The bed is covered in apple green with a cream quilt to match the beige carpet. The ceiling has been painted white, providing a contrast with the bold pink and blue, floral and peacock print wallpaper.

The adjoining bathroom boasts a huge corner bath set on a raised platform. In contrast to the brown and apricot bathroom suite, the remainder of the room has been decorated mainly in blue with ceramic tiles extending the length of the room. There is a touch of high tech in the white metal rack used for storage of towels, shoes and bottles. Appropriately, David Hockney motifs appear on the bathroom cabinet and a decorative model penguin adds the final touch to the arctic blue decor.

The couple find that their business commitments keep them fully occupied and the house as a result is designed to be easily run. They cannot bear clutter but admit that the house is a glorious mixture of space and chaos and there is still plenty of work to be done, such as the building of a studio for them to work in. The house is particularly noteworthy for its bold use of colours, many of which would normally clash, but seem to work well in the appropriate setting.

Living with a Touch of Eastern Promise

Above: Designed in the style of a mosque, this house was built on stilts to avoid flooding, and is made from reinforced concrete.

Below: One of the domes rises dramatically above the circular dining table.

Not everyone's home falls within the established conventions and one of the most unusual encountered could be that of a young London couple who made a first home for themselves in a unique riverside house, originally designed to look like an Egyptian mosque.

Described by its owners as 'basically a bungalow on stilts', the house was built in the early 1920s when it attracted considerable interest in the press. The present owners have inherited the carefully preserved old newspaper cuttings and faded photographs which record the construction of the house over a period of some three years by one Percy Stammwitz, who worked at the time for the Natural History Museum in London. Percy had had a distinguished career in the army during the Boer War and even took part in an antarctic expedition during 1913–14. As a result of his many and varied travels, the house he built is full of mementos, even down to its name, 'Arnussi', named after an oasis in the Gaza Strip.

Apparently, while working at the Museum Percy Stamm-

witz used to spend his lunch hours watching the workmen building an extension, which was one of the earliest buildings to be made out of reinforced concrete. His lunchtime observations influenced his own designs and aided by his teenaged son, Percy dug no less than a hundred tons of ballast out of the nearby River Thames with which to make concrete. This was then poured into moulds to form the 6 ft (2 m) high pillars on which the house now rests.

Fifty years later, however, the building's sturdiness failed to impress at least one building society, the owners recall. Apparently their surveyor who called to look the building over did not even bother to get out of his car but did a U-turn and returned to his office to write a letter turning down their application for a mortgage.

Undaunted, the young couple persevered and eventually found a building society willing to help them. Certain modifications were carried out, including changing the kitchen, and the couple did most of the work themselves.

This sun lounge runs the length of the house at the rear and is informally furnished. Giant cushions are used for seating.

As the single storey building rests on stilts, it was comparatively easy to get underneath to install pipes and wiring. However, the thickness of the concrete meant that these operations had to be carried out using a mechanical hammer, equipment that is necessary even if you wish to hang a picture on the wall.

Heating has been a considerable problem. The house was built without insulation and consists of solid walls. The couple eventually decided to install oil fired central heating, partly because there is no gas in the area due to the proximity of the River Thames. In carrying out the alterations they also found that the house had been built with true Eastern disregard for straight lines and right angles, as Stammwitz did everything by guesswork. Basically it is an approximate square shape, with a flat roof topped by three golden domes and two minarets, one of which doubles as a chimney. Climbing steps to the front porch, a visitor is at once struck by a moulding on the cement wall bearing the legend 'Arnussi, 1923', set in a desert scene of palm trees and camels. An elaborate screen covers the front door on which is carved the coat of arms of the Holy City—four black crosses empaled around a fifth larger one.

The entrance porch leads into the main front room of the house where a huge circular dining table stands beneath a vast dome. Somewhat incongruously, a pinball machine placed against the wall emphasises the present owners' 1980s tastes.

The owners have deliberately tried to get away from the mysterious East idea, and except for the original decorations, and there are many of those, they have used modern ideas throughout. The Eastern touches include a whole wall covered with hieroglyphics featuring a page from the 'Book of the Dead' in the British Museum, while from another wall Queen Nefertiti, Tutankhamun's mother-in-law, looks down.

Other parts of the house are reminiscent of the builder's Boer War experiences, with scenes of dancing girls and mysterious Eastern cities. A huge fireplace bears the motto of Mr Stammwitz's old regiment, 'For Home and Fireside'.

Leading off the main dining room is a smaller room which the owners use as their summer bedroom. This is in contrast to a small, windowless room situated in the centre of the house which they describe as their winter bedroom. This room is so narrow that they have raised the floor and put a mattress on it to form their bed. The result is an extremely welcoming nook, with the end wall painted black and an ornate carved mirror serving as a headboard.

Leading off the other side of the dining room is a bathroom. This is reached by a few steps leading upwards and is very simply decorated. It has a window in the ceiling which lets in

sunlight.

Because the building is without corridors, the kitchen has to serve as a link between the front and back of the house. Accordingly it is designed galley style, with modern units providing plenty of work space. Oven and hob are built in for easy running and a well stocked fridge and freezer stand on the opposite wall.

Beyond the kitchen and down a few steps is a sun lounge which runs the length of the house at the rear. This is casually furnished with giant cushions, hi-fi and television set. The steps themselves provide further informal seating and the huge windows look out onto green fields, giving the house a country feel even though it is in reality quite close to town.

All over the house there are small windows which have been let into the solid concrete walls wherever the sun can penetrate. The owners have done all they can to keep the house as it was originally built, and certainly the spirit of Percy Stammwitz lives on. Maybe the mummified cat who sits behind a glass panel near the front door is also wearing a satisfied grin these days.

This unusual house shows that with the right amount of determination and flair even an unconventional building such as this can be turned into a comfortable and interesting home for the 1980s.

Above left: The kitchen is, in effect, a corridor linking the front and back of the house. It is thus designed in galley style with modern appliances built in on either side.

Above right: The bathroom is just one of several rooms with unusually placed windows. These were inserted by the original builder wherever he saw that sunlight could enter.

Views of the bedroom and adjoining dressing room. The bed, consisting of a mattress on a raised floor, takes up the whole floor area of this windowless room—a cozy retreat for cold winter nights. The owners enjoy a second 'summer bedroom' during the warmer months.

Two
Clever Conversions

In the top flat a gallery overlooking the living room is a useful study area. This runs across the top of the bedroom and is reached by ladder.

When three young people get together to solve their accommodation problems, and one of them is an architect, then the results are likely to be different. In this case it was the transformation of a run-down terraced house in central London, that previously had been divided into numerous, small and distinctly colourless bed-sitting rooms.

The house had been owned by an elderly couple who had apparently done little decorating for many years. Many of their tenants had left and the property was generally run down. At the time, the three friends were living in furnished rooms in places like South Kensington and getting fed up with the usual restrictions that applied to rented accommodation. They were also motivated by the fact that the Greater London Council were offering useful improvement grants towards property renovation and the architect among the trio quickly submitted an application. This was not without its problems as the intention was to turn the property into three distinct flats and they had difficulties persuading the authorities not to treat the building as a whole and therefore only make over one amount of money. Looked at in this way the total sum would have made the project beyond the value applicable for a grant.

Eventually the architect was able to convince the local authority of the genuineness of his case and in an effort to save cash the trio moved into one of the spare rooms while the conversion work got under way. For several months they lived like this, often without heating and with only one cold water tap, preparing their meals on a small portable stove and somehow managing to survive. Builders were employed for the major structural work, but they soon found that their elaborate architectural plans were being ignored and found that drawing quick sketches on the back of an envelope was often the best way of explaining what they wanted.

The concept was to divide the house into three units, all of them self-contained. The basement was left more or less as it was, but the ground, first and second floors were divided into two sections, each providing a flat that takes up one and a half floors. The first of these is entered by a ground floor lobby and features a bedroom or study at this level. The room's size has been reduced to allow for a new separate stairway that leads to a first floor living room, a kitchen/diner and a bathroom.

The second flat is on the higher level and makes use of the original stairs which take you up to the first floor bathroom. Another short flight leads to a half landing into the kitchen and then a few more steps take you up to the second floor. Here the whole area has been opened up to the height of the rafters, providing a large open plan sitting and sleeping area, with a

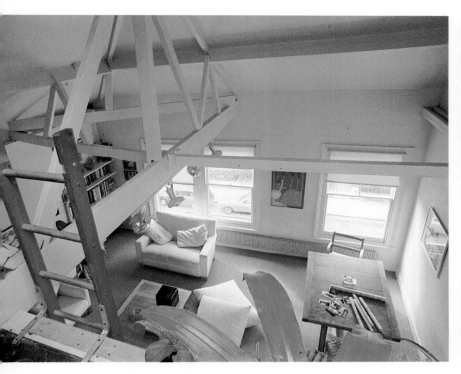

Two views of the open living area of the top flat, one seen from the gallery. The ceiling was removed, the exposed roof beams painted to match the walls and the roof insulated. Most of the furniture came from junk shops and has been modified to suit the owners; for instance the coffee table is a dining table with its legs sawn off.

small section above the bedroom converted into a study.

The two flats represent contrasting styles of décor, although there are linking features in the choice of textured buttermilk emulsion for many of the walls and the use of innovative ideas, such as neat, low level radiators instead of the usual obtrusive panels, and the incorporation of separate boiler units which supply hot water and heating to each flat. The young architect's connection with trade suppliers led him to the discovery of many useful industrial components that could be incorporated into the house. Floors are covered in natural coir matting and its use elsewhere helps pull the scheme together.

The top floor flat has plenty of light and space. The living area, which takes up the whole of the second floor, comprises an open sitting and dining area and, at a higher level, a study that nestles under the roof and is reached by a ladder. The bedroom adjoins, and can be opened up by use of a wall of folding doors.

The basic colour used is cream, on the walls and ceiling, including the exposed beams. The coir matting and plain calico blinds at the windows give an air of light and spaciousness.

Furniture has been selected mostly from junk shops and consists of solid thirties pieces—giant sofas and armchairs stripped to their off-white calico covers and a couple of large floor cushions. Books and records are stored on wooden shelves each side of the chimney breast and a cube system is built in to house smaller objects neatly.

83

The coffee table consists of a former dining table with its legs severely trimmed and contrasts with the uncompromising wooden dining table and chairs bought for a few pounds. Downlighters are used effectively over the bookshelves and spotlights show off the abundant plants and the occasional print or poster. The study area is lit by two huge roof lights made of reinforced perspex, which also afford access to the adjoining building in case of fire.

Pale beige walls and carpeting have been used in the adjoining bedroom, in contrast with a colourful patchwork quilt and boldly patterned curtains. The bed consists of a mattress at floor level and apart from a small table and a pine chest of drawers the remainder of the furniture is built in.

The landing and stairs leading down to the kitchen present a complete contrast. Here a royal blue has been used on the walls, which carry a striking display of prints and posters covering everything from the Olympic Games to Andy Warhol's Marilyn Monroe.

A kitchen is on the level below. This has been decorated in olive green, which covers the ceilings, walls and floor. White melamine units and white tiled work surfaces confirm that this is a no-nonsense kitchen.

Opposite top: The stairs down from the top flat are used to display pictures and mementoes. Royal blue paintwork is used to good effect with a variety of dramatic modern prints.

Opposite bottom: The kitchen belonging to the top flat has been furnished with spartan efficiency.

Below: The top flat bedroom is an example of floor-level living. The central heating boiler is housed in the cupboard on the right.

Opposite top: The ground floor bedroom also affords a work area for the owner, a stage designer. An uninspiring view is screened off by blinds.

Opposite bottom: More plants in abundance in the kitchen and dining area which leads off the main living room.

The owner has indulged himself a little in the bathroom. The ceiling is the same cream textured finish, but the walls are marbled in apple green. The bath, basin and toilet are in Pampas. Concessions to comfort are the warm cork tiles on the floor and double glazed windows, and a telephone extension to avoid racing up all those stairs to the living room.

Starting again at the ground floor, the other flat also occupies two levels. A cosy bedroom and work area have been constructed just inside the entrance hall, adjacent to the stairs that lead up to the living room on the first floor. The walls are apple green, the ceiling buttermilk and coir matting is used on the floor, as it is in the rest of the flat. A useful cupboard has been built in under the new stairway and a huge theatrical hamper gives a clue to the owner's profession as a stage designer. Some of his work is planned at the drawing board sensibly located close to the windows, where Venetian blinds filter the natural daylight. A folding decorator's paste table provides additional work space.

Below: This light and airy living room, belonging to the lower flat, is situated on the first floor. The plain blinds and pale cream walls are softened by an abundance of plants and the comfortable upholstery of the sofa and chairs.

Climbing the stairs, the living room is first glimpsed at worm's eye level, the effect being like climbing into a loft. Abundant windows admit plenty of light, supplemented by spotlights in the evening, and the plain blinds and bare cream

Scrunched up aluminium foil pasted on the walls and bath create an Aladdin's cave effect.

walls are softened by the use of plants and comfortable upholstered sofa and chairs.

Leading off the living room is the kitchen/diner. Here the floor is tiled in cork and the white and stainless steel kitchen units and sink have been neatly confined to an end wall, below the window. The dining area is finished with solid pre-war pieces, including a beechwood sideboard and open shelves for plants and kitchen objects above.

The bathroom is reached from a small hallway off the kitchen and here the owner has run riot. The formal suite is somewhat overpowered by the use of scrunched up kitchen foil pasted to the walls, ceiling and bathroom surround. The effect is dramatic, rather like being in an Aladdin's cave. The floor is cork tiled and a single downlighter and electric extractor fan complete the fittings.

Overall, the trio of occupiers are pleased with the results of many months of frustration during the building and alteration work. Certainly the results show just what can be done when three enthusiastic youngsters decide to do something different about their accommodation problem. Sitting high up in the airy living room of the top floor flat, it is hard to believe that you are really in a fairly ordinary street just a few minutes from a busy shopping centre and a trunk road carrying traffic west out of central London.

Thirties Influence in a Modern Setting

The search for their ideal home led the owners of this house to a former coach house set rather incongruously in the middle of a busy London suburb.

The house, for which a mortgage was granted only after all the conversion work had been completed, was originally built in the early 1930s when a larger adjoining property was extended. One obvious influence from this period is the Odeon-like front entrance which gives a small clue to the style of furnishings inside.

Basically of solid construction, the house is positioned at a low level in relation to the adjacent street, and as a result damp problems have had to be overcome. Conversion also involved a lot of work renovating the parapets and a flat roof, which now provides the owners with an elegant and practical garden.

Another aspect of the conversion work inside was the removal of partition walls to create larger open spaces from the cluster of original small rooms. For example, the present living room consisted of two separate rooms, while the kitchen has

Delightful decadence in the downstairs bathroom. The illusion of a sunken bath is created by covering the sides of the bath in carpet.

been made out of no less than four rooms, one a small w.c. Doorways have been cleverly blocked off or disguised, and it is difficult to detect any traces of the former layout. The result is a charming and unusual house.

On the ground floor there is an entrance hall with a bathroom leading off it, plus the spacious living room and kitchen. There is also a ground floor guest bedroom. Upstairs are the main bedroom, with its own bathroom, and a landing that leads to the roof garden.

In their choice of furnishings and décor, the couple have adhered to an interesting 1930s style, although there are distinct Hollywood overtones apparent, particularly in the living area.

The living room itself is a light, cool room, with a fine, natural wood block floor. American style wooden louvred shutters adorn the windows, and help to screen an unpromising view. Well cushioned ample sofas and chairs, one of which was rescued from the Biba store just before it closed down, continue

Cool blue decor has been used for the guest room on the ground floor. The window features American-style folding shutters for added privacy and security.

Above left: The natural, country style of this kitchen is achieved by concealing all the modern appliances behind a dividing wall. Second-hand pine floorboards have been used to make the doors and cupboards.

Above right: The spacious, cool living room is furnished in the style of the thirties with authentic pieces.

this style. There is a delightful mix of pink fabrics and cane, a huge palm tree and a distinctly pre-war drinks trolley, all contributing to the atmosphere and making this a soothing room with no evidence of any modern additions. It is literally like stepping back some fifty years or more.

The kitchen presents a complete contrast: here the owners have opted for a simple farmhouse style, achieved by using natural brick for the floor, white ceramic tile worktops, and secondhand pine floorboards for doors and cupboards. There is also a lovely old fireplace, while the main items of furniture include a solid pine dining table and benches, and a pine dresser. French doors lead directly to the garden. Even here, there is little evidence of modern appliances, as they have been partially concealed behind a brick room divider.

One of the most engaging features on the ground floor is the bathroom. Here the owners admit they felt the urge to go overboard in terms of décor. Walls and ceiling are finished in shiny black emulsion, contrasting with a vivid pink fitted carpet, which is also used to cover the bath surround and a series of steps up. This creates the illusion of a sunken bathtub. Huge mirrors and spotlights add a further splash of delightful decadence.

The ground floor guest bedroom has cool blues on the ceiling and walls and a darker blue carpet. The bedspread enhances this theme and once again American style wooden

Above left: Pink and green predominate again in the main bedroom.

Above right: Twin basins and mirrors contribute to the thirties feel of this bathroom which adjoins the main bedroom.

shutters are seen at the windows.

In a house that is already full of surprises the upstairs floor is a real gem. A spacious landing, painted white with pure white vinyl floor tiles, has been designed as an elegant sun room. Masses of plants and a low sofa/bed prepare one for the roof garden, which leads directly off through wide French doors. The whole view is reflected in a huge, wall hung mirror. A small table and canvas director's chairs double for use outside during the summer.

What is now the roof garden was one of the most neglected parts of the building when the couple moved in. They can only imagine that the previous owners were unaware of its potential. It was simply a flat roof, with a chimney from the living room, which they felt was crying out for something to be done. Accordingly they repaired the asphalt surface and then fitted part of the roof with raised wooden slats, ideal for sunbathing. The remaining area is covered in Astro-turf, artificial grass sometimes used for football pitches or tennis courts. Wooden trellis work obscures some of the harsher views and ensures a degree of privacy.

The main bedroom is at the back of the house. Here pale green walls contrast with the deeper green carpeting. French slatted blinds are used at the windows and a complete wall of pine cupboards contributes to the room's uncluttered feel.

Pink and green dominate the bathroom. There are twin

What was a spacious landing has been converted into an elegant sun lounge. The table and chairs can be used as outdoor furniture in the roof garden beyond the French windows.

Exterior showing the entrance with its Odeon-like architecture reminiscent of the thirties.

basins, a bath and shower cubicle, all in white.

The owners both have hectic jobs in the fashion industry and fashion journalism, so the resulting house offers a quiet retreat from the rigours of life in central London.

A Cottage Conversion in Cornwall

Converting a medieval barn into a series of cottages intended primarily for holiday use calls for very special skills. This conversion of a large building on a farm site in Cornwall is a good example of what can be done.

The buildings were probably the former manor house and one of the problems in attempting the conversion into a series of self-catering units, was to preserve the unique character of the building, in particular, the granite framed doorways and windows which occur on the courtyard side of the building.

Although the former barn had included an upper floor this was almost entirely within the roof space and in order to comply with current building regulations it was impossible to maintain this floor at its original level. To obtain the extra height needed, the upper floor level was lowered by some 2 ft 6 in. (75 cm). This solution enhanced the appearance of the ground floor area on the west side of the building but created problems on the courtyard side which was found to rest on a layer of top soil only, with the result that these walls required underpinning. It is problems such as these that make cottage conversion an exacting and exact science.

The owners also had to decide how to divide the large open barn into a number of units. There were basically three large open areas, which have subsequently been divided, and a former coach house which appears to have had some accommodation over it. Fortunately, the position of the original granite framed doorways allowed the builders to place two cottage entrance doorways set back inside each archway, providing separate access to six of the units, while the coach house section received slightly special treatment in order to preserve its unique character.

Large heavy pine beams recovered from an old London warehouse were used to span the length of the cottages and support the upper floors, with the addition of massive uprights spaced at intervals. The result has been an interesting open plan interior, comprising at ground level a living, dining and kitchen area, and on the first floor a bedroom and bathroom. Throughout finishes have been left natural, with use of pitch pine, and stone walls that have been either pointed or painted with white emulsion or simply left untreated.

On the ground floor the décor presents a number of interesting contrasts, with a white painted ceiling and two large cross beams and two uprights. One wall consists of rendered granite stone while the three others are painted white. A particularly attractive feature is the deep window sill made of pitch pine, the window itself overlooking a trout pond and stream. The owners' choice of furnishings is anything but 'cottagey' and

Above: Two views of the living/dining area. The dining table consists of a solid pine panel slung between an upright pillar and the end wall. The large cross beams were bought from a London dockland warehouse due for demolition.

the style adopted would suit any town house or flat. The floor is covered in a light brown carpet, and seating consists of a sofa/bed covered in natural canvas and two easy chairs in pine, with attractive brown and white check patterned cushions.

Although entered directly from the courtyard the living room has a number of levels, with the entrance a few steps higher than the rest of the room and providing a link with the stairs leading to the upper section. The half wall built here effectively delineates the seating area with its comfortable sofa, solid pine coffee table, pine bookshelves and colour television.

The kitchen is partially concealed by a counter some 5 ft (1.5 m) high, behind which are ranged a cooker and refrigerator, stainless steel sink and storage units in white melamine, with further use of pine where shelves can be seen from the sitting area. Bottled gas is used for cooking.

The dining table consists of a $1\frac{1}{2}$ in. (38 mm) thick piece of pine slung between the end wall and one of the upright pillars,

The wash basin in this bedroom is set into a solid pine dressing table so that it does not intrude into the room.

and is capable of seating six on wooden folding chairs. Spotlights have been used throughout, with the addition of a low enamelled shade over the dining table itself.

The first floor, which consists of a bedroom and bathroom, does not extend the full width of the cottage, and as a result light can pour in through a large window on a half landing and from a

The compact bathrooms illustrate economical use of space. All the pipes are hidden behind pine trunking matched by the mirror surround.

clerestory set in the roof.

The sleeping area, which is therefore visually linked with the ground floor, is furnished with spartan simplicity—comfortable double bed, covered in a cheerful duvet, and clothes storage confined to a curtained alcove. A washbasin has been added for extra convenience, but set into a solid pine dressing table it does not intrude into the room. The floor is close carpeted in dark brown and the walls are of rendered stone, painted white.

The adjacent bathroom and toilet demonstrate economical use of space, with a toilet, washbasin and shower cubicle grouped together in a very small area. Brown carpeting has again been used, against white walls, and service pipes have been concealed inside a pine box which runs up one corner of the room. A splash of colour is provided by the bright yellow door.

Sensibly the owners firmly rejected any of the clutter normally associated with traditional cottage furnishings. Instead they have made a good choice of natural fabrics and surfaces, and use of solid modern furniture throughout. The result is undoubtedly pleasing to the eye and manages to combine warmth and comfort with the minimum of housekeeping. Given the nature of the intended occasional use of the cottages, and the distraction afforded by the countryside close at hand, this represents an admirable compromise.

A Large
Family House

This large family house belongs to a well-known film maker. Situated in a leafy suburb it is called, incongruously, the Little House, although in reality it is quite large with no fewer than forty-nine windows to clean! Parts of the building date back to the 1780s, but inside the owners have avoided harking back to the Georgian origins of the house, and the décor and furnishings represent a happy compromise between good, solid pieces of traditional furniture and some nice modern touches. All blend together with a totally unfussy style of decoration which is very fresh and relaxing.

The house is required to perform a number of functions, apart from providing a comfortable home for the owners and their family. Much of the husband's work is done there in a comfortable study retreat, and they also like to entertain. Fortunately, most of the rooms are well proportioned and on the ground floor the hall, living room, dining room and kitchen all conveniently link together.

The decorating scheme chosen is used to unify the con-

The main lounge is traditionally furnished, with a large open fireplace and comfortable upholstered settees and chairs. Note the arrangement of framed pictures on the wall, unifying the collection of different sized objects.

stituent elements of the house. For example, the use of plain cream walls and white painted ceilings in most of the ground floor rooms, wood block floors extending from the hallway into the living room, and quarry tiles laid in both the dining room and the kitchen.

The living room itself is simply and comfortably furnished, the main elements being two large sofas upholstered in dark brown cord material, which face each other on either side of the open fireplace. The fireplace is tiled and surrounded by an attractive carved mantle and dominated by a substantial framed mirror. Two large windows are set either side of the fireplace, shielded by wooden slatted blinds. A mirror and period pictures take up most of one wall.

There is a small study corner for answering the telephone and writing letters. The room is lit by wall mounted brass lamps.

The dining area represents a change of period, with the accent on quarry tiles and natural pine, and in fact this part of the house is a later extension. Large arched windows made from

The dining room, situated in an angle between the living room and kitchen, is reached down a short flight of steps. There is ample space for entertaining here with a fine view of the garden through the arched windows constructed out of screens from a film set.

Opposite top: The luxurious and elegant bathroom with white tiled and dark coloured walls matches the colour scheme in the bedroom.

Opposite bottom: More than just a bedroom, this is a room to relax in away from the hurly burly of the rest of the household.

Below: The large, well appointed kitchen, with plenty of storage space, adjoins the dining room and is handsome enough to be seen from the dinner table anytime.

several old screens taken from a film set, face the garden. The rectangular dining table is made of pine and surrounded by eight plain, cane seated bentwood chairs. A pine dresser displays an attractive collection of colourful china, and another is used to display photographs relating to the owner's work.

The dining area is approached by steps down from the living room and there is another slight change of level with one step up to the kitchen, which opens out from the dining room. Here natural materials have been used throughout, with quarry tiles on the floor, white ceramic tiles on the wall, and solid marble work surfaces. Storage units are made of pine that has been stripped and stained and there is a mixture of drawer units and open shelves to house kitchen paraphernalia.

Concessions to twentieth century living include an amply sized stainless steel sink, dishwasher, and combined refrigerator and freezer. Sensibly, laundry equipment has been confined to a separate utility room and this lovely kitchen presents the appearance of an old fashioned grocery store rather than a busy modern work area.

There is also a smaller sitting room on the ground floor, which is used for informal occasions and for watching television.

Upstairs are bedrooms for parents and children, two bath-

rooms and a study. Because the principal bedroom has windows on two sides, the owners felt able to choose darker colours, relieved by occasional splashes of colour in the patchwork bedspread and white painted woodwork.

The carpet is brown shag pile and walls and ceiling are covered in dark brown patterned wallpaper, with the design repeated on roller blinds at the windows. Clothes are stored in a specially made unit of rich mahogany, which itself is complemented by a beautiful old oak chest. The fireplace surround is painted white and features a cast iron wood burning stove, also painted white. In contrast, the doors of the bedroom and of the adjoining bathroom are of stripped pine.

Brass wall lights have been hung over the bed and dressing table, the latter with a solid marble top. This comfortable retreat also has its own television and hi-fi.

The bathroom has the same carpeting, wall and ceiling coverings, with white ceramic tiles forming a splashback behind the bath and basin. The cupboards and bath surround are of stripped pine, the w.c. seat of mahogany.

The various children's bedrooms are full of bright cheerful colours, with white paintwork that can be easily cleaned or repainted. Toys are stored on white open shelves or in pine

The owner's work room is equipped for film editing and writing. The theme is black and chrome, creating an elegant retreat where serious work can be undertaken.

chests of drawers. Zany drawings appear on the walls of the children's own bathroom, which is dominated by a large notice announcing that 'The Management Requests you to Scrub all over'.

The first floor study makes dramatic use of black and white. Ceiling and walls are painted white, with a black dado running around the walls. The woodwork is all painted black as is the desk with its chrome legs. Chrome is repeated in the cane seated desk chairs and a leather and chrome framed sofa. There are numerous built-in shelves for hi-fi, film reels and a typewriter. A director's folding chair and film editing machines are clear indications of the owner's occupation.

The result is a comfortable family house, without a hint of ostentation. It is also one in which children are always welcome. They like the fact that there are lots of stairs and hiding places, and they regard the second sitting room as very much their own.

By the use of natural materials such as marble and rich woods, and the employment of colours that unify the house's different parts, the owner's simple approach has enhanced the grandeur of this lovely old building.

Traditional
Country Style

Above and opposite top: Two views of the ground floor living area which has been divided into a number of separate zones for conversation, playing cards around a splendid poker table (**above**) and watching television. The room has been furnished with solid classic pieces.

Opposite bottom: The panelled and beamed dining room boasts a sixteenth-century fireplace and with the dinner table set and candles lit, it is easy to slip back three hundred years in the imagination.

This delightful period house is set in rural Oxfordshire and disguises a fully functional modern interior, designed for timeless elegance.

When the owners acquired this rambling house, they were undaunted by the problems they expected to face and firmly decided upon a style of living that they intended to create for themselves.

They were determined to make the house feel their own, and to do this had to cope with several practical problems. These included a mixture of styles and floor levels, and practical problems such as the gales of wind which blew through $\frac{1}{4}$ in. (6 mm) gaps around many of the windows. These were later cured by fitting double glazing neatly inside the existing frames, so that the attractive casement windows are not affected when viewed from outside. This sort of treatment typifies the owners' approach to the rest of the house.

Major work included installation of central heating and hot water, and several changes in the layout of various rooms. This involved dividing up bedrooms for the children and creating a bedroom, bathroom and dressing room for the owners' parents.

The owners were assisted by a professional interior designer, who is more at home when designing hotels or airport lounges. There are perhaps several hotel-like influences in the bedroom and bathroom, which serve to enhance the overall appeal of the house.

The interior, although carefully coordinated, combines a mixture of styles, perhaps in keeping with the house's varied history of additions and embellishments over the years. Outside, the exterior is best referred to as Tudor-Bethan. On entering the house, one feels a great warmth of welcome, for the spacious hall is furnished with deep red leather chairs set before an open fire, with a leather topped club fender. There are panelled walls and low ceiling beams, and this is very much a place best enjoyed on dark winter evenings. Standing in a corner, to add to the cheerful pub atmosphere, is an upright piano.

The dark brown carpet of the hall extends into the main living area, helping to unify the various ground floor areas and to compensate for abrupt changes of level. The colour has also been chosen for its resistance to children and dogs.

The main living room presented a number of problems because of its size and shape—a long rectangle which culminates in French doors overlooking the garden. Sensibly, the owners have divided this room into three basic sitting areas: one just inside the door around a low coffee table, just the place for after dinner gatherings of friends; a second one ranged around

long comfortable sofas that flank the fireplace; and a third which is a games area near the French doors, the centrepiece of which is a splendid poker table.

White emulsion has been used on the walls and ceiling, with colour provided by the patterned curtains and abundance of cushions on the sofa. Recessed spotlights provide overall illumination, which can be adjusted, and complementing this are a number of handsome table lamps.

Good solid pieces have been used throughout this well proportioned room, and there is a marked absence of clutter. Ornaments, hi-fi and other objects are consigned to sturdy shelves built into an alcove next to the fireplace.

The panelled and beamed dining room, perhaps lends itself best to formal occasions. When set with traditional silver cutlery, beautiful china and candles to illuminate the scene, one could be forgiven for dreaming of meals that must have been consumed here several centuries ago. Further illumination is provided by adjustable wall lights and a barbeque has been built

Designed like a hotel bedroom, the owner's room has space for taking breakfast, listening to music and watching television. The wall-coverings, coordinated with bedspread and curtains, are made of fabric stretched on wooden frames.

into the large open fireplace, which dates back to the sixteenth century.

The principal bedroom and its adjacent dressing room are large, extending as they do over the ground floor living area. A number of functions are catered for here, in addition to sleeping and dressing, making these rooms rather like a suite inside a top grade hotel. As well as containing a king sized double bed, the bedroom itself is comfortably furnished for watching television, listening to hi-fi or relaxing over a leisurely breakfast served at an elegant round table set in front of the bay window. The owners like to think of this room as a retreat from the hustle and bustle of the rest of the house and thoroughly enjoy its multi-functional purpose.

The décor is pretty and feminine, with patterned fabrics used for curtains and covers. On the walls themselves a light material has been stretched on battens and used as a wall covering. The process is French in origin and is rather like stretching canvas on a picture frame. As well as compensating

The dressing room adjoining the main bedroom has a rather theatrical air. These units are made in ash and have been stained to bring out the grain.

A bathroom, also adjoining the main bedroom continues the same colour scheme.

for considerable unevenness in the original wall surfaces, it improves the resonance of music from the hi-fi speakers by reducing bounce.

In the separate dressing room the built-in wardrobes are made of ash and treated with an interesting grey stain that enhances the appearance of the wood. The units, which contain ample mirrors, were purchased as standard. There is also a large desk here for attending to correspondence and accounts.

The bathroom is glamorous enough for any film star. Natural materials such as marble and cork have been used to great effect. An archway leading to the bath alcove and the use of a dado give a thirties impression which is still further enhanced by the use of tungsten bulbs around the dressing mirror. The whole area is covered in luxurious shag pile carpet.

Very little has been done to the traditional farmhouse tiled kitchen, which boasts a north facing pantry and original tiled floor discovered beneath a layer of linoleum. This room is functional rather than decorative.

Faced with the problem of a number of clashing architectural styles, unpretentious and straightforward solutions have been found with no attempt to add any false glamour to the building. Structural alterations have been kept to the minimum and the result is an old world charm combined with the very best design influences from France, Italy and America.

Close Enough
for Comfort

This smallish living room, entered direct from the street, is given a visual extension through the use of mirrors behind the alcove shelving on either side of the fireplace.

Town centre flats are very expensive, but then so is the cost of commuting. This house is a charming compromise, a small terraced home that is close enough for comfort.

Holding down a full-time job as director of a public relations consultancy and having to look after one small son meant that the owner had to choose and design her home with several requirements in mind.

After a succession of flats in central London, she was longing to buy a house of her own, and as she was firmly set against the idea of commuting she needed to be close to the centre but had to find a home that was within her price range.

A judicious sale of her former flat, which she decorated and put on the market at the start of the property boom, enabled the owner to buy a small terraced house in South London, not far from a common and little more than half an hour's drive from her office in Kensington.

The house is situated in the sort of street that estate agents like to consider 'improving', and consists of a large ground floor through living room, a dining room and kitchen. The kitchen was a later addition to the property and occupies most of what was formerly the garden. Upstairs is a large bedroom and a balcony for her young son, the balcony extending over the whole of the new kitchen extension. There is also a large main bedroom with a bathroom en suite. On the second floor is another smaller bedroom and a second bathroom.

The house was the usual collection of small rooms, the owner recalls, with an entrance hall which she felt took up too much valuable space. So the dividing wall was removed, the whole of the front part of the house opened up, and the lounge extended towards the rear of the building.

The effect has been to create a comfortable sitting area, built around a splendid Victorian fireplace that delights visitors as soon as they come through the front door from the street. Draped curtains are used effectively to help soften the lines of the newly created gap and form a visual barrier between the entrance and the living room.

The end wall of the hall, another new addition, blocks off the view of the stairs that formerly confronted you as you came through the front door. This and the arrangement of the seating in the lounge have helped to preserve at least a feel of separation between the entrance and the seating area.

Arranging the furniture in the living room was a difficult problem. The owner brought some furniture with her when she moved and for several months tried out different combinations but found she simply could not get it right. She tried various suggestions of friends before achieving the final result which

consists of two large sofas grouped around the fireplace and close to the television and hi-fi unit, providing a cosy seating area that is perhaps best enjoyed on long cold winter evenings.

The floor has been covered in dark brown carpet tiles and the walls are covered in a pale lemon shade, with the mouldings delicately picked out in white. Deep red patterned fabric is used for the curtains at the pleasant bay window and for the cover of one of the sofas. The other is in off-white sheepskin.

Wall mirrors have been set into the alcoves on either side of the fireplace and help create an illusion of space, reflecting plants, china and other objects arranged on plate glass shelves.

The rear part of the lounge is still not fully furnished. The owner would like to buy a piano or other fine piece of furniture to complete the area, but she has not made the mistake of rushing to buy anything that would simply fill up the space.

The dining room is situated towards the back of the house and adjoins the newly built kitchen. This is an ideal arrangement as the owner does quite a lot of formal entertaining at home and chose a large dining table that can comfortably accommodate up to eight guests.

Here the colour scheme is beige—carpet tiles are again used on the floor, and the beige curtains are bordered in dark brown. The walls have been covered in an intriguing patterned paper in brown and cream, and beautiful Victorian style wall and ceiling lights complete the warm, nostalgic atmosphere.

Above left: Another view of the living room showing the front door. A dividing wall has been removed to create more space and several seating arrangements were tried until this combination was decided upon.

Above right: The dining room prepared for formal dinner. Beige carpet tiles are used on the floor.

Below: Modern cupboards and work surfaces in the kitchen require the minimum of maintenance.

Above: This cheerful boy's room has plenty of space for playing and masses of cork covered wall on which to pin junior artwork and posters. The French doors lead to a rooftop play area.

Below: The cramped bathroom is given a splash of colour with cool green painted walls.

Presenting something of a contrast, the kitchen is designed for ease and efficiency, with a gleaming worktop in woodgrain laminate and handsome dark brown wall- and floor-mounted storage units. A patterned cushioned vinyl has been used on the floor and the walls are tiled. The units have been arranged in a horseshoe shape, with natural light and a view of the garden through a large window. A sliding door gives access to an outside paved area.

Moving to the first floor, her son's bedroom has been tiled in cork so that pictures and drawings can be easily pinned up.

Cool greens and blues have been used for the remaining bedrooms and bathroom, and in the smaller bedroom, co-ordinated wallpaper, curtains and bedcover help draw the scheme together.

By using colours cleverly and sensibly, confining different sections of the house to basic browns and creams, the owner has succeeded in unifying the diverse elements that go to make up this compact and welcoming home.

Right First Time

Opposite left: The tiny kitchen has been cleverly furnished with built-in cupboards and worktops. There is even space for a fold-down breakfast table.

Below: Light and colour enter the hall through carefully preserved multicoloured glass windows. The woodwork has been stripped of paint to reveal natural textures.

This comfortable small house, situated on the outskirts of London, typifies what can be done when a young couple get together and apply a certain amount of flair and hard work to the project of getting together their first home. Before they got married, the young owners had no clear idea of what they wanted to buy, nor were they drawn to any particular area of London. However, they did prefer somewhere broadly within a central area and a location that would reduce the time spent travelling to work to a minimum.

Beyond that they had no preconceived ideas and spent many fruitless weeks looking in areas that clearly were unsuitable. After a number of disappointments, including nearly completing the purchase of a house that fell through (almost literally) after an adverse surveyor's report, they found what became their present home in a pleasant suburb close to a park. This has turned out to be the ideal location, with property values nearby continuing to rise, and potential for considerable extension of the house should they decide to stay there for a long time. A number of houses in the street have been extended either upwards or outwards into the garden, and these were important factors that contributed to their decision to go ahead.

As with many older properties, the building was in a state

of disrepair. As the owners recall, an old lady had lived there for many years and not very much work had been done to the house. However, the couple liked the position, at one end of a peaceful road with plenty of trees, and close enough to shops and park.

When they moved in, the house consisted basically of two ground floor rooms and a small kitchen, with three bedrooms and a bathroom on the first floor. It has taken considerable imagination to visualise what could be done to turn the house into exactly what the couple desired.

Enlisting the help of their family and friends they first began the task of clearing the accumulated rubbish and forgotten furniture, and stripping down the walls and paintwork. They next considered a number of alternative plans for the ground floor, and were undecided on whether to link the kitchen with the rear living room using an archway or door, or to knock the two living areas into one and leave the small kitchen as it was.

Above: Two ground floor rooms were opened up to provide a large living/dining area, comfortably carpeted and furnished with lasting items such as the leather Chesterfield.

Below: Heavy, dark curtains matching the carpet add warmth and luxury.

119

They finally decided on the second solution and, using ceiling supports hired locally, they knocked down the dividing wall. The doorway into what had been the front room was also blocked off and plastered over.

Removing this central wall meant that a supporting column had to be built with foundations reaching into the basement, on one side of the room. The ceiling is now supported by a rolled steel joist which rests on a pillar at one side of the room and on a special concrete lintel inserted into the party wall of the house next door. This operation was carried out with some professional help but is one that can be quite easily accomplished by do-it-yourself builders.

The couple also decided to install full central heating and simply gut the existing kitchen and bathroom. Accordingly an old coke boiler, a metal storage cistern, a sink and washbasin, w.c. and heavy enamel bath were all removed and transported to a crowded skip, next to the lead and copper internal pipes that had been pulled out. It was at this stage that the couple experienced some of the panic associated with this kind of operation, asking themselves whether they would ever succeed in getting the house together again. They were literally left without plumbing, with the exception of one cold tap, and many of the operations had left gaping holes in various walls and ceilings. However, they decided to press on.

The kitchen was a particularly awkward problem because of a tiled floor that sloped badly, and there was also a rather dangerous step down from the hall, a drop of some 6 in. (15 cm). To cure both problems at once, they decided to raise the floor to the same level as the hall by laying hardcore and then concrete, which was subsequently relaid with fresh quarry tiles. This cosy theme has been continued through the kitchen with the use of deep red patterned tiles behind the sink and work surfaces, and the use of warm pine for the kitchen fitments. Situated in a corridor between two doors, the kitchen can become quite cold, but this has been cured by installing the central heating boiler in one corner, and relying on it to heat the room. The couple also installed a simple drop-down table for breakfast and snack meals taken in a hurry.

The work of rewiring, plumbing and installation of the central heating system was efficiently carried out by a combination of Gas Board workers and a further batch of willing friends. Within weeks of their wedding the upstairs rooms were more or less habitable and the main bedroom ready for occupation.

Looking back on the transformation that they effected, they realised that they learnt a great deal in the process. One of the best things they did, they recall, was to decorate and sand

floors as they went along. Although some walls that they painted were eventually covered in paper and floors that had been sanded were later carpeted, in some cases this happened as much as a year after they had moved in, and the couple were quite happy to live in this unfinished state until they could afford the furnishings that they wanted. Even after a couple of years the house was not completed as the owners sometimes took a rest from building and decorating just to enjoy the place. However, holiday weekends have been spent painting the outside woodwork, replacing roof tiles and clearing out the garden. They now have plans to build a patio and possibly a conservatory extension.

The illustrations best convey the style of furnishings adopted by the couple. Throughout the ground floor they eventually laid a thick pile dark brown carpeting, covering the whole of the living area and the entrance hall. Contrasting with this are the pale pastel colours of the walls and ceiling, although the

Above left: The bedroom doors have also been stripped of paint and the same dark brown carpet has been used throughout the hall, stairs and landing.

Above right: It was difficult to fit basin, W.C., and bath into this small bathroom after the old fittings had been removed.

This quiet rear bedroom has a fine view of the garden. The tiled open fireplace has been retained as a feature.

heavy dark curtains at either end of the living room add further touches of warmth and luxury. A large black slate fireplace became the centrepiece of the main living area, having been moved there from the other end of the room. This, in effect, is quite a simple operation.

The couple are still getting together some of the movable furniture, and decided to buy good quality items as they went along. One of their major investments was a luxurious leather chesterfield sofa, while much of the rest of the furniture was picked up at bargain prices from junk shops and antique stalls. A pine dresser at the far end of the living room was rescued from beneath many layers of white paint.

The brown carpeting is continued upstairs and on to the first floor landing and bathroom, but in the two bedrooms the couple have chosen a beige carpet, which offers a pleasing contrast. Pastel colours are also used again, and added warmth results from use of stripped pine on all the room doors. Both bedrooms have attractive open fireplaces. A third, smaller bedroom has been converted into a small study, where the owner keeps his typewriter and large collection of books.

The bathroom is quite small and presented considerable problems arranging the fitments in position. The bath is full size and the walls surrounding it are tiled to shoulder height so that at a later date a shower can be added.

The couple are generally pleased with the results of their efforts and certainly they have succeeded in creating a comfortable home, with room for expansion at such time as they start a family.

Deep in the
Heart of the Country

Above left: A fireplace of truly immense proportions is the dominating feature of this room, which is actually known as the small sitting room.

Above right: The main living room runs through most of the house and has the kitchen, other rooms and stairs leading off. Another huge fireplace provides heat and ventilation.

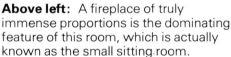

Opposite top: Detail of one of this house's many open fireplaces which the owners have restored to its near original state.

Opposite bottom: One of the bedrooms, furnished with heavy wooden pieces in keeping with the style of the home.

This 400-year-old farmhouse is set in the heart of rural Huntingdonshire and is the home of a London couple who forsook the bustle of city life and opted for the peace and quiet of the country.

The decision to move was not a sudden one. For a period of some eight years the couple had looked for that elusive country cottage and had concentrated their efforts among the remote hamlets of East Anglia. What they finally saw and eventually purchased was a Tudor farmhouse whose condition could only be described as derelict and in dire need of a major transformation. However, the setting was right, away from towns and villages, and yet near enough to London for the period that they would have to continue working in the city and commute to their new home in the country.

The building is fairly typical of its period, basically built around two enormous fireplaces whose chimneys dominate the rooms on the upper floor and warm up the whole building when in use. The foundations are not what one would expect to find today and the ground floor ceiling tends to sag towards one end of the house, but this is quite common in buildings of this age.

Built of stout timbers and stone, the farmhouse is remarkably solid, although considerable restoration work had to be undertaken over a period of some four years.

Major work included rebuilding the front wall and restoring mullioned windows. Inside the house, several old fireplaces

Warm pink and beige colours have been used in this bathroom. Again the beams have been left exposed and a thick shag pile carpet gives warmth underfoot.

were found to be blocking the original chimney breasts. These were cleared away, revealing enormous alcoves supported by solid timbers in which huge logs cheerfully burn today.

On the ground floor there is a main hall with a large fireplace at either end. Off this lead a small comfortable living room with its own fireplace, a former back house converted into a small picture gallery and dining area, and a modern bathroom with adjacent kitchen.

One end of the ground floor area would normally have served as a typical farmhouse kitchen, but the owners felt that they could make better use of the space by opening up a partition wall and integrating the area within the rest of the ground floor. When they are not entertaining guests, they make use of the second living room with its pleasing mixture of original old beams, the rich patterned carpet and traditional upholstered armchairs.

The main hall provides another seating and dining area, although guests are sometimes entertained in the picture gallery which would formerly have been the dairy and outhouse of the farm. Leading off this is a study, used for quiet work.

The kitchen is best described as workman-like and has been relegated to the back of the house, although a useful serving hatch connects it with the gallery area during meal times. The kitchen itself is well concealed behind a traditional oak door.

An important concession to comfort is the downstairs cloakroom, equipped with a shower cubicle and a washbasin. It also serves as a drying area for clothes, although the couple planned an extension to the house which would include a laundry and drying room.

Upstairs are four bedrooms, a bathroom and dressing room. As all the rooms intercommunicate in the style of houses of this period, privacy for guests is achieved by using a small hatch in the ceiling of the main downstairs hall and a solid oak stepladder to give access to the ground floor cloakroom without passing through any of the other bedrooms.

The upstairs rooms are covered in dark brown, close fitting carpet, which contrasts well with the timber beams and white walls and ceilings and creates an air of continuity. The couple's own bedroom and main guest room feature welcoming old fashioned double beds that militate against early morning rising during the winter months.

The bathroom is finished in warm tints of beige and pink, with luxurious shag pile carpeting underfoot. Heating the house is by use of the traditional open fireplaces, supplemented by electric radiators.

Those who think that such surroundings would lead to a relaxed country lifestyle would be surprised to learn that the couple rise at six each morning and have a full working day. Before breakfast they have chores to perform, including feeding and exercising goats, collecting logs for the open fires, sorting out washing and food, and looking after their young children.

However, the house has provided them with a spacious home and place to work and is in marked contrast to the crowded city flat that they willingly left behind.

Above left: One of the four comfortable bedrooms in this house. Part of the major restoration work involved the replacement of all the windows.

Above right: A former back house has been converted into a small picture gallery which provides yet another area for entertaining.

Index

Page references to illustrations are in *italics*.